DRUGS AND PEER PRESSURE

Peer pressure exists in many different settings, including the pressure to excel in school.

THE DRUG ABUSE PREVENTION LIBRARY

DRUGS AND PEER PRESSURE

Arthur Myers

THE ROSEN PUBLISHING GROUP, INC.
NEW YORK

To Virginia Ritchie Cutler

Published in 1995 by The Rosen Publishing Group, Inc.
29 East 21st Street, New York, NY 10010

First Edition

Library of Congress Cataloging-in-Publication Data

Myers, Arthur.
  Drugs and peer pressure / Arthur Myers. — 1st ed.
    p.   cm. — (The drug abuse prevention library)
  Includes bibliographical references and index.
  ISBN 0-8239-2066-6
  1. Drug abuse—United States—Juvenile literaure.
2. Drug abuse—United States—Prevention—Juvenile
literature. 3. Teenagers—Drug use—United States—
Juvenile literature. 4. Peer pressure in adolescence—
United States—Juvenile literature. [1. Drug abuse.
2. Peer pressure.] I. Title. II. Series.
HV5809.5.M94   1995
362.29′12′0835—dc20   94-37885
                                                   CIP
                                                    AC

Manufactured in the United States of America

Contents

It takes a lot of courage to say no to your friends.

CHAPTER 1

Just Being a Teenager Is a Pressure Situation

Cheryl wanted to fit in.

She was 14, a freshman in high school. Maggie Klein had invited her to a party, and that was something! Maggie was a year older, but she had sort of taken Cheryl under her wing by inviting Cheryl to a party at her house.

When Maggie opened the door, the party was already under way. Cheryl shyly followed Maggie around as she introduced her to the other kids. Most of them were juniors; a couple were seniors. Cheryl blushed when Bill Collins, a center on the basketball team, smiled at her. He had a can of beer in his hand.

"Hi," he said, "would you like a beer?"

No, she thought, she wouldn't like a beer.

8 | *Her father drank beer a lot, and she had secretly tried it. It was so bitter. How could anybody drink that stuff? But her mother drank it too, sometimes. And most nights her parents would have a cocktail. They weren't alcoholics, but they drank.*

For the past few years, teachers, counselors, parents, and police officers visiting the schools had lectured on and on about the dangers of alcohol, smoking, drugs, sex— maybe even crossing the street without look-ing both ways. But most of the adults she knew did some or all of those things.

And she desperately wanted Bill Collins, Maggie Klein, and everybody at this won-derful party to like her.

"Thanks," she said, when Bill popped a can open for her.

Peer pressure can be as simple as that. A mild suggestion from somebody you want to like you. No twisting of arms, no sneers, no threats. Just the unspoken message—You want to be cool, you want to belong to our clique? Then do what we do.

We all want to *belong*, whether we admit it or not. It doesn't matter what age we are, what period of life we are in. There are cliques in schools, offices,

country clubs, prisons, old-age homes. **9**
But nowhere are cliques, sets, gangs,
crowds—whatever you want to call
them—so important as they are in high
school. That's because the people in high
schools are teenagers, adolescents.

Being an adolescent is a tough time of
life, no matter what you hear. There are
adults who tell teenagers, "This is the best
time of your life." People who say that are
spreading false information. Adolescence
is usually one of the most difficult periods
of life.

Why is being a teenager so tough?
Because change is tough. Change can
cause more stress than anything else. And
adolescence is *the* time of change. Big
change, fast change. When you were 12,
you were a cute little kid. Five short years
later you're a young man or woman, with
the body of an adult, whether you like
that body or not. It's a confusing, often
frightening world.

Your attitudes change. Your parents are
no longer gods. In fact, sometimes you
wonder if you even like them anymore.
You need them—and then again, you
don't need them. You're sorting out the
values they've handed you. Some you
agree with, others you don't. There is a

Using drugs can foster a sense of acting like an adult.

big do-as-I-say-not-as-I-do factor in what they hand you. They may drink, smoke, go through red lights. But don't *you* do that!

So you hang out with the other kids, people in the same boat. It's us against the know-it-alls, the adults. What the heck, we're adults ourselves—almost. And of course, you are right.

What's an easy way to act like an adult? You're not really ready to do brain surgery, or audition for the lead in a major motion picture. But smoking, drinking, using pot, or popping pills can be a temptation. It's easy. You don't need any skill to do it. And it feels good—at least temporarily. The catch is that you can get hooked on it. And then it feels absolutely rotten.

Of course, nobody wants to admit that he or she is subject to peer pressure. One high school counselor says:

"You ask young people if peer pressure influences them to cheat, or drink, or do drugs, and most of them say 'Nah!' They're thinking, if I say peer pressure influences me, it means I'm weak, I can't make up my own mind."

But we're all subject to peer pressure, whatever our age. If you're 40 years old

12 | and the only one on the block who doesn't cut the lawn, you're in social and psychological trouble. So you cut the lawn. We're all influenced by others.

A social worker whose clients are troubled teenagers, many with drug or alcohol problems, points out that we live in a drinking, drug-using society. Kids are bombarded with TV and movies that show substance use and abuse. Magazine ads feature happy beautiful people smoking and drinking. The message is that that's how they got happy and beautiful.

A psychologist says that anti-addiction programs in schools hit the kids' brains, but not their guts. No teenager wants to become an alcoholic, or a dope addict, or to wind up with AIDS, probably contracted when under the influence or by sharing needles. But it's hard for a kid to translate a puff on a cigarette or a joint, or drinking a beer or two, into trouble down the road.

Adolescence is a time of experimentation. Teens play with their personalities. "Who am I today? Who will I be tomorrow?" Experimenting with your personality is fine as long as you remember that you are always accountable for your actions. Trying drugs is no exception. Addiction holds a steep price.

Even adults are subject to peer pressure, such as that connected with the appearance of the home or yard.

Experimentation cuts across gender, cliques, and social and economic class. Sometimes the facts are surprising. Some counselors and kids say that inner-city kids are less likely to become heavily into drugs and alcohol because they see the consequences—the drunk in the gutter, the heroin basehead next door. These end-of-the-line people are more hidden in the suburbs. They're around, but they stay indoors.

It doesn't matter so much what crowd you run with in school. One social worker says:

Drug use occurs among teens of all social groups.

"I can think of a kid in trouble with drugs or drink for every clique you can imagine. The kids who are great students and hard-working. The kids who are dying their hair purple and dressing wildly. The kids who are juvenile delin- quents. The kids who are athletes. The kids I worry about most are the average students, the kids who look like they're doing so well but who are drinking like crazy. They are the social group. They grow into adults who are the most social, unquestioning of the social order. They're the people who fit in. Our culture is drenched with alcohol. How many people have a party without alcohol, or dinner without a drink? And there's also a lot of marijuana in these so-called clean-cut groups."

This social worker has worked with kids in all of these high school groups when drugs and alcohol have been a problem. Their grades slip, they fight with their parents, they've gotten into a car crash after drinking, they've gotten into fights, they've had sex when they didn't want to after drinking, they've made fools of themselves, their girlfriends or boy-friends are concerned and are pressuring them to look at what they're doing.

When kids get to the point of cutting most of their classes, fighting with teach-ers, acting erratically, showing great anger and irritability, they're almost always heavily into drugs and alcohol.

To most teenagers today, drinking and drugs are glamorous. They represent adult behavior, they represent experi-mentation, which is tempting. If you can't resist these new toys, it might not be a bad idea to listen to some of those vaguely revolting people over 30— adults—who are trying to come up with a safety plan for you.

CHAPTER 2

Fun or Poison?

Most people don't think of alcohol as being a drug. But it is.

A few glasses of beer, a shot or two of whiskey, a cocktail—pretty much the American way of life. Kids, immersed in an ocean of TV shows, movies, newspaper, magazine, and billboard advertising, have alcohol drummed into their eyes and ears many hours a day. It's hardly surprising that soon many kids start using the product.

It's not hard to get. It feels good at first. It relaxes you. It gives you a high.

It also makes you sick. It's habit-forming. It makes you act foolish. It can be deadly.

You can take your choice of fatal possi-

It is difficult to ignore the pull of advertising such as this.

Drinking is often a learned behavior.

bilities: quick death via an alcohol-related auto accident or fight, or slow death by cancer, cirrhosis of the liver, or other deadly ailments.

Keep on drinking, and you'll damage your brain, your liver, your heart, or your stomach. Or all of the above. Booze can be fun—till it grabs hold.

Drinking has increased among young people in recent years. Nicotine and other drugs are down a bit, because of the avalanche of negative publicity against smoking and heavier drugs. But drinking has a particular appeal to teenagers

because so many adults do it. It's not as

scary as the other drugs. It's relaxing—to start with.

People who work with teenagers—guidance counselors, teachers, social workers—estimate that some 70 percent of high school kids drink casually. They do it mostly on weekends—the Thank God It's Friday routine. They're copying many of their elders.

High school is high pressure—both academically and socially—and alcohol is a way to forget problems for an hour or two. Then they come flooding back, along with headaches and guilt. And worse.

The Party

Let's pick up Cheryl, who went to the glamorous party of the popular group. She's desperate to stay in with them. Cheryl's parents are away for the weekend, so she throws a party. Everybody gets drunk. They couldn't imagine a party without liquor. It's the norm.

Cheryl gets quite drunk. Before long she is upstairs with Bill Collins, the basketball star. Any one of a number of things could happen from here.

- Bill sobers up filled with remorse for having persuaded Cheryl to have sex

20

even though he knew she didn't want
to.

- Cheryl sobers up and is pregnant.
- Bill or Cheryl sobers up with an STD,
  a sexually transmitted disease.
- Or, a short time later, Bill or Cheryl
  tests positive for HIV (human immunodeficiency virus), the virus that is
  believed to cause AIDS (acquired
  immunodeficiency syndrome). This
  may be a worst-case scenario, but
  statistics indicate that by the year
  2000 a frightening 40 percent of
  college students may be HIV-positive.
  And teens are the most rapidly grow-
  ing group at risk for HIV and AIDS.

Kids begin drinking at younger ages
than ever before, some even in junior
high school.

*Jerry Mancini was 13. One winter
Saturday afternoon he went to a diner with
some friends. Among them was his best
friend, Ted Elliott. As the boys sat drinking
their milkshakes, Ted's older brother, Frank,
came in with a friend. They sat with the
younger boys. Gradually the two older boys,
who were 18, began kidding the younger ones
about drinking milkshakes.*

"They're babies," Frank said to his friend.
*"Maybe we ought to get them started on
the right stuff," the friend said.*

*The younger boys piled into Frank's car
and headed for the Elliott home. The Elliotts
were away—it was a chance for a party.
Frank stopped at a liquor store and bought
several six-packs of beer.*

*The boys played video games. They drank
the beer. They even copied the older boys and
tried chugging, swallowing it down fast. Soon
a couple of kids got sick. Frank drove them
home, although he himself was drunk. They
were lucky. They made it without getting into
an accident. The younger boys, however,
drunk and sick, had to answer to their parents.*

*Jerry Mancini was not so lucky. He
staggered outside by himself and wandered
around to the back of the house to throw up.
He sat down in the snow. He passed out. It
was 5 degrees above zero. Two hours later, a
man reading gas meters went around behind
the house and saw Jerry slumped in the snow.
Jerry was very still. He had frozen to death.*

Nicotine

Another drug that can be deadly is nicotine. Like alcohol, nicotine—which for
teenagers usually means cigarettes—is not
usually thought of as a drug. After all, it's

legal, it's common, it's advertised. But it *is* a drug—in fact, it's the No. 1 killer drug in the United States. Almost 400,000 people die from smoking every year in the U.S. Yet every day more than 3,000 teenagers light up for the first time and launch themselves on a journey to painful diseases and shortened lives.

Statistics say that after age 20, every pack of cigarettes can shorten your life by 137 minutes. Nicotine clogs your blood vessels, shortens your breath, and causes deadly breathing diseases such as emphysema. Studies indicate that smoking increases women's risk of dying from breast cancer. It can cause lung cancer, and it's harmful to your heart.

You don't necessarily have to *smoke* tobacco to get its bad effects. Chewing tobacco—so common and publicly visible among professional baseball players—can give you mouth cancer.

Cigarettes are one of the most heavily advertised and promoted products in America. This heavy advertising is backed by billions of dollars from tobacco companies. It is fueled by greed. Their view is that money matters most, and that the health of millions of people is relatively unimportant.

The smoking industry puts most of its advertising dollars toward the effort to hook young adults.

However, a concerned public is fighting back. In recent years, laws have made it more difficult and expensive to smoke. Voters have placed heavy taxes on cigarettes. Smoking is restricted in most public places.

There are fewer and fewer smokers. At one time, it was easy to get a light. Almost any adult—in the office, in the elevator, on the street, at home—carried matches or a lighter because almost everyone smoked. Today, few people carry matches or cigarette lighters—or cigarettes.

But the cigarette industry sees young people as fair game. They are the tobacco

Cigarettes are sometimes called a gateway drug—a lure into using stronger drugs.

trade's hope for the future. The Joe Camel promotion is specifically aimed at youth. Cigarette ads feature attractive, athletic young people. And now, with the U.S. market showing signs of slipping, the tobacco interests are setting their sights on foreign markets, particularly on the youth of Third World countries, where education is less extensive and the young people may be less aware of the dangers of smoking.

Cigarettes and beer are sometimes called gateway drugs. From them, people often move on to marijuana, and then to harder drugs.

Marijuana

The fact that marijuana has so many af-
fectionate nicknames—"pot," "Mary
Jane," "grass," "weed"—indicates how
seldom people fear it. Just an occasional
harmless puff. But for some, it often
turns out to be not so occasional—and
not so harmless.

It's a mood-altering drug made
from the hemp plant, *Cannabis sativa*. It
becomes particularly dangerous when
taken, as it often is, with alcohol. The
effect is tripled. Pot, beer, and driving
have added up to many fatal road
accidents.

Among regular users of marijuana,
sore throats and eventual lung damage
are common. And health problems can
mount up in less obvious ways. For
example, pregnant women who use marijuana risk having a premature or low-
birthweight baby.

Regular pot smokers show a loss of
motivation. They tend to "drop out," to
lose interest in activities that formerly
interested them. They change friends,
drifting toward people who are also into
drugs. They often lose their former
friends. They are subject to mood swings
and irritability. Their attention span

Many people think smoking pot is harmless. However, pot has several long-term effects.

shortens, and they seem constantly distracted.

Jose Hernandez is an example of what "harmless" pot can do. Jose was a junior in high school. His relatives, his teachers, his fellow students admired him. His marks were high. He was often elected to class office. His parents dreamed proudly of his being the first in the family to get a college education and go on to a professional career. He wanted to become an aeronautical engineer, and he had already caught the attention of executives at a nearby airport. They had offered him a summer job as a technicians' helper.

But the job, so important to Jose, also caused him a certain amount of anxiety. He felt that everyone expected a great deal of him. He dealt with that by increasing his use of pot. Soon he was stumbling around the hangars in a marijuana daze. He became less and less aware of safety.

Jose wore glasses, and one day he wandered directly under the whirling blades of a helicopter that was taking off. He didn't lose his head, but he did lose his glasses. They were sucked up into the chopper's blades. The crewmen pulled him away, and Jose escaped physical harm. But he became a laughing stock. His superiors decided he was an accident waiting for a place to happen, and a few weeks later he was eased out of his job.

Jose was devastated. His answer was more pot. He went back to school for his senior year, but he could not concentrate. His marks nose-dived and he did not even graduate. He did not go on to college to become his family's first professional person.

Jose's experience with the copter was a joke to many people, a funny story at the airport and at his school. It wasn't funny in Jose's life. It was a tragedy.

Cocaine and Crack
You can die fast or slowly from these

28 poisons. Here's an example of fast.

Len Bias was the greatest basketball player in the history of the University of Maryland. A senior, he had just signed a contract with the Boston Celtics, one of the top teams in the NBA. At 20, he was about to become a millionaire. He flew back to Maryland, and that night was celebrating with friends. Len tried cocaine for the first time. A few minutes later, he was dead.

Cocaine is sold in two forms: a white powder and crystals. The crystal form is called crack. It is said that in the U.S. between 5 and 15 million people use cocaine regularly, and another 5,000 try it for the first time every day.

It's in schools. A therapist says, "I haven't worked with any kids who admit taking cocaine or crack, but a lot of them do. A hit of crack is only about $5, less than the price of a movie, so it's easy to start. Of course, if they get hooked the habit costs plenty. A heavy crack habit can cost $500 a day."

Cocaine is usually "snorted" up the nose. This is tough on the nose. Continued use can punch a hole in the septum between the nostrils. The "high" or "rush" is quick. So is the "crash." Chronic users become depressed and find

Cocaine is almost immediately addictive.

it hard to sleep. The drug is highly addictive. To support the habit, some turn to robberies and break-ins. Others borrow money and never return it. Shoplifting becomes a way of life. So does time in prison.

Cocaine users can undergo panic attacks and hallucinations. They are convinced that someone wants to kill them. They hear footsteps when no one is there. They see snakes winding around the bedpost. Cocaine affects the brain and can cause brain seizures, resulting in convulsions and strokes. Young people, even teenagers, suffer heart attacks.

Crack is cocaine that has been made into white crystals, which can be smoked. It is sold in small chunks, or "rocks." Sometimes it is sprinkled into a cigarette or a marijuana joint. It is a concentrated form of cocaine, and it is extremely dangerous and addictive. A crack high lasts five or ten minutes. The "crash" is very rough, leaving users tired, depressed, and irritable. "With crack," says a high school girl, "you go up, and then come *way down*."

After the rush, the user wants more crack immediately to get back up there. Crack is very hard to quit.

Crack addicts find the drug much more important than food. One high school boy using crack lost 40 pounds over a period of six months. "You just feel ugly," he says. "You don't want to look in the mirror, because you know you look disgusting."

Heroin

Heroin comes from the opium poppy, which is grown in warm parts of the world. Heroin is only one of the chemicals that are derived from opium. It is sold in the form of a whitish powder. It is quite expensive. Some users sniff it, but most inject it under the skin with a hypodermic needle. The most desperate addicts inject it directly into a vein. This is called mainlining. Addicts usually inject many times a day, which can cause veins to collapse. An addict then uses another vein, which results in "track" marks on his body. An addict sometimes misses a vein. This can cause an infection.

Mainlining is dangerous because needles are often passed back and forth among addicts, which increases the risk of getting AIDS.

Heroin sometimes makes a new user feel sick, but it can also produce a powerful "high," followed by a sense of relief from stress and worry. But it takes larger and larger doses to get the high, till eventually there is no pleasure at all.

But you're still stuck. Withdrawing from heroin is extremely painful, both mentally and physically. The addict who is withdrawing experiences anxiety, sleeplessness, desperation, and a terrible craving for the drug.

Not many teenagers use heroin, but they *can* eventually reach the stage of heroin by way of the milder drugs, such as alcohol and marijuana. And heroin is not completely unknown in high schools. One student said:

"People think you're a basehead if you

32 | use heroin. Especially if you shoot up.
But many kids in this school have people
in their neighborhoods or families who
have that addiction. It's scary. The ques-
tion kids keep asking themselves is—
'How can I stay away from this, what can
I do so that I don't get hooked?' "

Amphetamines and Barbiturates

Two types of widely used medical drugs,
often prescribed by physicians, are also
"street drugs"—sold illegally by drug
pushers—which can be very dangerous.
They are amphetamines, often called
"uppers," and barbiturates, termed
"downers." The uppers are stimulants,
the downers are depressants.

Amphetamines are sometimes called
"greenies," because the capsules they
come in are often green. This drug can
also be obtained as powder, which is
"snorted." Or it is injected by needle—
which involves a risk of AIDS. Uppers
provide a powerful high, an excitement
and energy. They also provide confusion,
inability to sleep. They can cause brain
damage or heart attacks. Many people
have died from overdoses. And mixing
uppers with alcohol is taking a chance on
death.

Using amphetamines and barbiturates can put your body on the roller coaster of sleepless nights and exhausted days.

The downers, barbiturates, are powerfully addictive. Withdrawal from these substances is even more difficult than from heroin. Sudden withdrawal can cause severe convulsions, sometimes death. Downers bring about a dreamy, relaxed state. They can also cause nausea, slurred speech, slow reflexes, double vision, and lack of balance and coordination. There is very little difference in the amount that produces sleep and the amount that kills. As a result, many people die from barbiturate overdoses every year.

33

34 | *Inhalants*

Use of inhalants is a type of substance abuse sometimes indulged in by children. It was popular in the 1970s and now seems to be making a comeback in middle schools and even the upper elementary schools. It is said that one in three children have tried inhalants.

What are inhalants? Certain types of glues and household products give off fumes that when breathed provide a kind of intoxication, somewhat like drunkenness. Further sniffing can cause dizziness, confusion, and often aggressiveness. It can produce hallucinations, resulting in panic. These chemical fumes, which can come from model glue, cleaning fluids, paint sprays, and gasoline and kerosene vapors, are mind-altering. Kids who get high on these solvents can be involved in violence or have accidents. They can suffer serious burns, for sometimes these substances explode in flames. Some users have suffocated when using plastic bags to concentrate the fumes. Others have passed out and choked to death on their own vomit. Inhaling from aerosol cans has caused many deaths of children and young adults.

Hallucinogens

Another type of substance abuse involves hallucinogens. Such drugs are termed psychedelic—which means mind-expanding. A widely used psychedelic drug is LSD, short for lysergic acid diethylamide. It is also known as "acid." This substance was very popular back in the 1960s, in the days of communes, rebellion, and Flower Children. Some of today's teenagers romanticize the '60s, and "dropping acid"—swallowing the drug on a sugar cube or a very small tablet—can seem like part of the '60s game.

An LSD "trip" refers to a particular mental state, often involving hallucinations. Sometimes the visions are beautiful and truly seem to be mind-expanding in one way or another. But as with all these drugs, there is also a dangerous downside. Sometimes the user experiences a bad trip, frightening and unpredictable. One can panic, become violent, get involved in accidents. An especially scary characteristic of LSD is that flashbacks can occur without further doses. A bad LSD trip is nothing anyone would want to repeat—but it can happen spontaneously for years afterward.

36 Another substance that was popular in the 1960s and is becoming popular once again are psychedelic mushrooms. In the '60s they were called "magic mushrooms." Today they are more commonly known as "shrooms." These mushrooms contain a drug similar to LSD. Eating them can make a person hallucinate, see and hear things that aren't there. As with LSD, a user risks experiencing bad trips.

Another danger in using psychedelic mushrooms is eating the wrong kindof mushroom. It is difficult to distinguish between psychedelic mushrooms and poisonous ones. Eating the wrong kind of mushroom can result in serious illness or even death.

A drug often mistakenly included in the category of hallucinogens is PCP, or phencyclidine. PCP is actually produced in laboratories. Also known as "angel dust," PCP is sold in two forms: as pills and as powder. The powder is usually snorted. It usually makes users feel passive or disconnected. It can also cause episodes of violent behavior, rubbery legs, dizziness, nausea, and feelings of terror.

CHAPTER 3

How to Say No And Still Look Cool

*T*here's something about starting high school. Something exciting, something confusing—but most of all, something scary. And something happens to kids as a result.

A teacher in middle school put it this way:

"The kids have been given information on drugs and alcohol and smoking, and they vow they will never get involved in such things. But something happens from the time they leave eighth grade and they enter high school. All of a sudden they've forgotten about all the things they said they would never do. They're doing them."

It's that thing called peer pressure.

37

You might find it easier than you think to turn down the drugs or alcohol your friends may offer.

We all need emotional support, approval from those around us. Few of us can be happy if we're isolated. It's especially hard to be alone if you're in high school.

At 13 or 14, you say goodbye to childhood and hello to adolescence. It's an uneasy hello. The teens are not a period most adults would like to return to. It's rough duty. Everything is new. It's a mad scramble for security. When you are plunked down into high school, three quarters of the kids are older than you, bigger than you, and wiser than you. At least that's what you think.

You really don't know for sure who you are. One minute you think you're invulnerable, nothing can hurt you. You'll live forever. The next minute you're frightened of this new life, this new body, this new place. You're excited by your growth, mental and physical, by your new sexual energies. You're filled with their promise of pleasure and joy—and the threat of pain and danger. It's all new, and if you weren't a little scared you'd be crazy. But teenagers are risk-takers, so you experiment, you explore what's out there.

Many ninth graders drink. They have many role models—a sizeable percentage of the adult population and a considerable percentage of the upper-class students. Some younger girls become sexually active, sometimes trying to become popular with older boys. Some ninth graders start smoking cigarettes, some smoke pot. Some try other drugs. It's a time of change, of stress, of reaching out desperately to settle into this new life, this new identity. It's a time of doing whatever you think needs to be done to be liked.

It's easy for adults to say, "Just say no." But it's not all that simple. Often, there is nobody in particular to say not to. Except, perhaps, yourself. It comes down to a

40 matter of self-esteem, of what you think of yourself, what values have been built in by family, community, friends. The bottom line is your own particular personality and character.

We're all different. We're not all strong, we're not all independent. Most of us are a long way from being self-sufficient. It's easy to tell young people, don't let it bother you, don't worry what other people think, be your own person. Sounds simple, but it's not. Many of us have a need to *follow*, to do what others do, to try to make others like us, to avoid rocking the boat. Not many kids are strong enough to be indifferent to what the other kids think. But there are ways to handle situations, and here are some scenarios that may help.

Margo

Margo had gone on a day of biking with her friends Kim and Janet. At noon, they pulled over to a rest stop and unpacked their lunches. When they had finished eating, Margo was surprised when Kim pulled out a pack of cigarettes, shook out one for herself, and gave one to Janet. She turned to Margo and said, "Want one?"

Margo had never smoked. She had no

Standing up for yourself by not following the crowd may strengthen your self-esteam.

desire to. She had seen her grandmother die slowly and painfully from emphysema, a disease often caused by smoking. Granny had been a two-pack-a-day smoker. The last two years of her life she had been unable to breathe without an oxygen tank and had been barely able to get around. This was not for her, Margo had decided.

"No, thank you," she said.

The other girls lit up, and Margo hoped that was that. But it wasn't. Her friends were obviously angry. They felt rejected. They also probably felt guilty.

After a few puffs, Kim turned to Margo and said, "You're so boring."

41

42

It was like a slap in the face. Margo had known these girls since they were in elementary school. She felt tears well in her eyes, but blinked them back.

"Sometimes she can be fun," Janet said, "but sometimes . . ." She let the sentence hang. Margo felt as though she too were hanging, that their friendship was hanging in the balance.

"She's so afraid her mother will kill her," Kim said, taking another puff.

"One cigarette, big deal," said Janet coaxingly.

I feel betrayed! Margo thought. These girls are supposed to be my friends!

"You're such a baby," Kim said.

Then Margo began to get mad. She wasn't going to take this lying down.

"Why are you picking on me?" she asked.

"What do you mean, picking on you?" Kim said. But her voice was a bit unsteady. She seemed a little unsure of herself.

"You're making fun of me, calling me a baby, that's what I mean!"

"Don't take it so seriously," Janet said. "Don't get mad."

"Okay," Margo said, "I won't. When you've finished your smokes, let's hit the road again."

And that's what happened.

What Margo had done was reverse the pressure, and it worked. It worked because people usually want to be your friends as much as you want them to be your friends.

In fact, usually they think better of you if you stand up for your rights.

Sherell

Sherell had just moved to town and hadn't formed any strong friendships yet. One afternoon as she was coming out of school, she heard her name called. Looking around, she saw a girl called Annie, who was in her English class. Annie was sitting in a convertible. Two other girls and three boys were in the car.

"Sherell, wanta go for a ride?" Annie called.

Sherell was in the car instantly.

She felt great riding around with the top down, the wind in her hair, everybody laughing and yelling at kids on the sidewalks. So she was surprised when one of the boys said, "Are we having fun yet?"

She sure was. What did he mean?

"Let's have a real party," one of the other boys said.

"Hey," said one of the girls, "my parents are on a trip, wanta come to my house?"

44   *"Got any good stuff there?" asked the boy who was driving.*

"You mean booze?" laughed the girl. "We've got oceans."

Sherell soon found herself in the family room of a large house. The boy who had asked for a "real" party was pawing through a huge refrigerator. He pulled out two six-packs of beer and yelled, "Let's send this party into orbit!"

He turned to Sherell, ripped a can of beer from its package, and said, "You're Sherell, right? Here, have a beer."

"I don't drink beer," Sherell said. "Is there some soda in that fridge?"

A groan went up.

"A sissy," one of the boys said, "we've got a sissy."

"A party pooper," one of the girls said.

But another girl, whom Sherell recognized from her history class, said, "Aw, give her a soda. It's a free country."

The girl went to the fridge, found a ginger ale, and handed it to Sherell.

Sherell was relieved when everybody started dancing. It took the pressure off her, as she stood there with her can of ginger ale.

She danced with a couple of the boys, but she wanted to remove herself from this situation as soon as possible—gracefully. She went

to the hostess and said, "Hey, this is fun, but **45**
*I've gotta leave. My little brother's baby-
sitter leaves at 4:30 and I have to fill in till
my folks get home."*

*This wasn't completely true, but she felt it
was one of the smaller lies she'd told in her
life. At least, she wasn't hurting her hostess's
feelings.*

*Going down the sidewalk, she heard her
name. It was the girl who had given her the
ginger ale.*

*"Hi," the girl grinned, "my name is
Connie. Do you really have a little brother?"*

"Yeah," Sherell laughed, "but he's 12."

*"That was a good way to get away from
that crowd," Connie said. "You didn't make
any enemies. I wish I had done something
like that. I didn't have the guts to turn down
a beer. I didn't know what to do. But you
stood up for yourself without spitting in any-
body's eye."*

*"I'm new here and I'm looking for
friends, but I'm not sure that's the right
crowd for me," Sherell said.*

Connie nodded. "Listen, let's get together."

"Catch ya later," Sherell said.

A lot of kids want to say no when
they're offered alcohol, nicotine, and
drugs. You're not alone. Many *do* say no.
There are many ways to say no. It's good

Sometimes the best way to avoid your friends' drug use is
to leave.

to remember that above all, you are your
own best friend.

Jim

*Jim was only 13, but he knew his own
mind and wasn't afraid to speak it.*

*Jim's older brother, Wade, had taken him
along for a tennis afternoon with Wade's
friend, Mike. After an hour of banging the
ball around, they strolled over to a tree and
plopped down in the shade. Mike fished some
marijuana from his pocket, rolled a cigarette
and handed it to Wade. He made one for
himself. He asked, "Should I make one for
the kid?"*

Wade said, "Sure, it's time he got into the
act. You'll have a joint, right, Jimmy?"

*Jim wished he could disappear. But he
couldn't figure out how to do that. So he
said, "No, thanks."*

*"Okay, Skipper," said Wade, and he and
Mike began to puff away and chat about
their girlfriends.*

Sometimes that's all it takes—a polite
no.

It's certainly worth a try.

But sometimes that doesn't work. So
here are some other options:

Suppose Wade and Mike had kept at
Jim. Jim could have kept on saying no
and have worn them out.

Wade probably would have finally said
sarcastically, "I don't think he wants it."

Jim would have made his point, and
that would have been that.

Jim had enough self-esteem to refuse
to do something he didn't want to do,
and the older guys respected him for it.

You can do that, too.

Of course, the world is filled with people who want everybody to like them.

It's also filled with people who want to
force their will on others. It's called hus-
tling somebody. People like this try to
make their "friends" feel there is some-

48 thing wrong with them if they don't do what the hustler wants them to do.

You've got to learn to do what *you* want to do, not what somebody else wants you to do.

These hustler types don't hustle you as much as you *let yourself* be hustled.

If they get too bothersome, tell them a joke.

Change the subject. Say, "Let's go to the movies," or "Let's go to the mall and play video games."

Say, "Forget it."

Say, "See ya sometime," and walk off.

Do *your* thing. It's a free country.

And of course, don't be a hustler yourself. Don't try to persuade other kids to drink, or smoke, or do drugs. When you do that, you're just trying to persuade *yourself* it's okay. You're trying to cancel out your own feelings of guilt. And it doesn't work. You'll probably end up feeling worse.

And don't be what the counselors call an "enabler." An enabler is a person who enables—or helps—another person go the wrong way.

Here are some examples of enabling:

• A high school boy is constantly get-

Be prepared for a strong response if you decide to confront a friend about his or her drug or alcohol use.

ting the answers to homework from a friend who is a brain. She doesn't like giving him the results of *her* work. She knows he never has the answers because he spends much of his time in a drug fog. But over and over she gives in. Finally, enough is enough. She works up the courage to say no and refuses to give him the answers. Actually, she has done him a favor.

- A girl calls up another. The conversation goes like this:

   "Sally, this is Ruth. I've got a huge favor to ask."

Your friend will most likely be grateful for your help one day.

"What's that?"

"I was out last night with Billy. His folks are away, and when we got back to his house we got into the liquor cabinet, and did we get smashed!"

"So?"

"Well, I was so plastered that I didn't want to go home. So I stayed over at Billy's."

"And . . . ?"

"Honey, could I tell my folks I stayed at your house? They'd never check it out."

"Yeah, we hope."

"I know they won't. They don't even know your folks."

"Well . . ."

"I swear I'll never ask you again."

"Okay, this once."

What Sally has done for Ruth is enable her drinking. That was no favor.

- Jack is trying to borrow money from his friend Chuck. This has gotten to be a constant thing. They grew up together, played baseball and basketball together on school teams. Jack has dropped out of sports, and Chuck knows it's because he's too involved in drugs to have the time or stamina to participate. Chuck knows Jack is going to blow the money on booze or pot.

  And yet, they've been friends so long that Chuck hates to refuse Jack. But he's not doing Jack a favor. Chuck is acting as an enabler.

It's hard to say no to someone you like. It's hard to feel like a friend when you turn someone down. But that is exactly what you *are* being—a good, loyal friend. There are ways to go about it,

Identify the problem by letting your friend know that you care about him and that you are worried about him.

ways to say no, yet not break up the friendship. Here are some of them:

- Explain why you won't do this favor. Tell your friend that you know what he is into, and that you just can't continue helping him or her ruin health and life.
- Let your friend know that you care, and that you're worried about him. Put your cards on the table. Identify the problem.

    "I know you've been smoking pot for months, and now I hear you're

getting into crack. Listen, don't you
realize that can be suicide?"

- Let your friend know that you are
there to help him in other ways.
  "Hey, let's go on a bike trip up
into the mountains, like we used to."
Or, "A bunch of the guys are getting
a summer ball club started. We sure
could use you as a pitcher."
- If you have to, just walk away. But
let your friend know this needn't be
final. Let him know you'll be there
to help if he calls on you. Leave the
door open.

Don't demand too much of yourself.
It's your friend's life, not yours. If your
friend is getting involved in drugs and
you feel you should help him, you should
never feel that you *have* to get involved,
or feel guilty if you don't want to. Your
own safety is just as important as his.

Be aware of the limits of what you can
do. If your friend is hostile or violent, or
in trouble with the law, is being abused,
is very depressed and talking about
suicide—don't try to handle it alone.

You might try to find out what professional help is available in the community.
There are probably counselors in your

54 | school you could start with. Advise your friend along these lines. Offer to go along with him if he wants you to. Being referred by and possibly accompanied by a friend can make things a lot less scary.

And don't expect too much. Your friend may reject your help. The counselors call it denial, and it happens a lot. No matter what happens, you shouldn't feel guilty. You don't have to get involved in your friend's problem if you don't want to. But if it feels like the right thing to do, you might use some of the helping skills you've learned in this book.

Most of all, be confident enough to do what you really feel. You might help save your friend's life.

You might save your own.

CHAPTER 4

Where to Find Help

*W*hen you have a problem—particularly an embarrassing one such as drug or alcohol dependence, or a sexually transmitted disease—it is often difficult to approach someone in person. It can be hard to talk with people you know, such as your parents, a teacher, a school counselor, or even your friends.

It is sometimes much easier to take that first step by talking to an anonymous, faceless stranger—someone you don't know, can't see, and who can't see you. This person should be able to give you expert advice on how to go about seeking help. Whatever the problem, help is only a phone call away.

The 800 numbers below are toll free. If

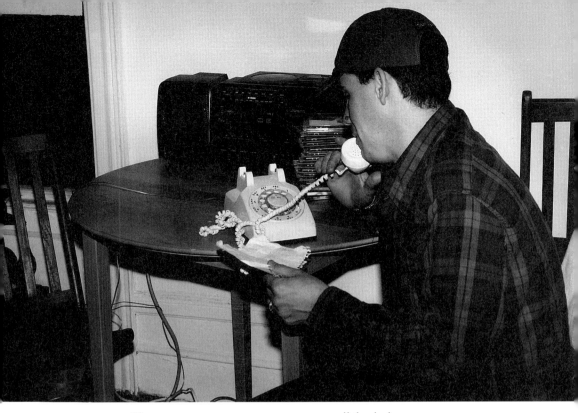

There are many resources you can call for help or more information about drug and alcohol abuse or addiction.

a number has a regular area code, it means there will be a charge. But if it's a place you think might help you, go ahead and pay the toll. It's a lot cheaper than the drugs or alcohol you've probably *been* spending your money on.

Addresses are also given if you can't bear to call.

Al-Anon/Alateen Family Group Headquarters
PO Box 862, Midtown Station
New York, NY 10018-0862
212 302-7240

This organization, designed for families and children of alcoholics, is connected to the famous Alcoholics Anonymous. It has chapters

all over the world. For information on meetings
in the US, call 800 344-2666.

Alcohol and Drug Problems Association of America
1555 Wilson Boulevard, Rosslyn, VA 22209
703 875-8684

Alcohol and Substance Abuse Program Branch of
the Indian Health Service
2401 12th Street NW
Albuquerque, NM 87102
505 766-2115

Cocaine Anonymous
6125 Washington Boulevard
Culver City, CA 90232
310 839-1141

Hispanic Information and Telecommunication
Network
449 Broadway
New York, NY 10013
212 966-5660

Institute on Black Chemical Abuse
2616 Nicollet Avenue South
Minneapolis, MN 55408
612 871-7878

Jewish Alcoholics, Chemically Dependent Persons
and Significant Others
426 West 58th Street
New York, NY 10019
212 397-4197

National Asian Pacific Families Against Abuse
301-530-0945

58 *Calix Society*, a Catholic society that sponsors
help for alcoholism
612-546-0544

Just Say No International
2101 Webster Street
Oakland, CA 94612
800 258-2766

Mothers Against Drunk Driving (MADD)
511 East John Carpenter Freeway
Irving, TX 75062-8187
214 744-6233

STOPP (Students to Offset Peer Pressure)
PO Box 103, Dept. S
Hudson, NH 03051-0103

SADD (Students Against Driving Drunk)
Box 800
Marlboro, MA 01750
508 481-3568

*National Clearinghouse for Alcohol and Drug
Information*
800-729-6686

Drug Abuse Information and Treatment Referral Line
1-800-662-HELP
(Spanish) 800-66-AYUDA

*Centers for Disease Control's National AIDS
Clearinghouse*
800-458-5231

STAT (Stopping Teenage Addiction to Tobacco)
800-998-7828

Glossary
Explaining New Words

Al-Anon Organization of men and women whose purpose is to support family members of alcoholics.

Alateen Support fellowship for teenagers who have parents with drinking problems.

alcoholic Person who is suffering from the disease of alcoholism, who has lost the ability to control drinking.

Alcoholics Anonymous Organization of alcoholics, whose purpose is to give each other support in avoiding alcohol.

AIDS (acquired immunodeficiency syndrome) Fatal disease, usually spread by sexual contact or by exposure to contaminated blood though hypodermic needles.

60 | *convulsion*   Intense, uncontrollable
contraction of muscles.

counselor   Person trained to give
mental and emotional advice.

emphysema   Serious disease of the
lungs, often caused by smoking.

hallucination   False perception of
objects or events, often as a result of
drug use.

HIV **(human immunodeficiency
virus)**   Virus that is believed to
cause AIDS.

joint   Cigarette made of marijuana;
sometimes called a reefer.

peer   Person who has equal rank with
others in age or status, as among
adolescents.

psychedelic   Type of drugs that cause
hallucinations and other changes in
one's states of feeling and awareness.

self-esteem   Pride in oneself;
self-respect.

substance abuse   Use of addictive substances, such as drugs and alcohol.

For Further Reading

Berger, Gilda. *Addiction*. New York:
   Franklin Watts, 1992.
———. *Making Up Your Mind about Drugs*.
   New York: E.P. Dutton, 1988.
Buckalew, M. W. Jr. *Drugs and Stress*.
   New York: Rosen Publishing Group,
   1993.
Campbell, Chris. *No Guarantees*. New
   York: Macmillan, 1993.
Chomet, Julian. *Cocaine and Crack*. New
   York: Franklin Watts, 1987.
Cohen, Daniel and Susan. *What You Can
   Believe about Drugs*. New York: Evans
   and Co., 1987.
Condon, Judith. *The Pressure to Take
   Drugs*. New York: Franklin Watts,
   1990.

62 Cretcher, Dorothy. *Steering Clear.*
Minneapolis: Winston Press, 1982.

Feller, Robyn M. *Everything You Need to
Know about Peer Pressure.* New York:
Rosen Publishing Group, 1993.

Friar, Linda, and Grenoble, Penelope.
*Teaching Your Child to Handle Peer
Pressure.* Chicago: Contemporary
Books, 1988.

Hurwitz, Sue, and Shniderman, Nancy.
Drugs and Your Friends. New York:
Rosen Publishing Group, 1993.

Johnson, Gwen, and Rawls, Bea
O'Donnell. *Drugs and Where to Turn.*
New York: Rosen Publishing Group,
1993.

Kaplan, Leslie S. *Coping with Peer Pressure.* New York: Rosen Publishing
Group, 1993.

Myers, Arthur and Irma. *Why You Feel
Down and What You Can Do about It.*
New York: Charles Scribner's Sons,
and Atheneum, 1982.

Ward, Brian. *Drugs and Drug Abuse.* New
York: Franklin Watts, 1987.

Index

About the Author

Arthur Myers is an experienced investigative reporter who has won several prizes for newspaper writing and who at one time was an editor on the *Washington Post*. He has published some 20 books, about half of them for young people.

Mr. Myers lives in Wellesley, Massachusetts.

Photo Credits

Cover by Michael Brandt; all other photographs by Yung-Hee Chia

Design by Blackbirch Graphics